CEREMONIAL

CEREMONIAL

poems by Carly Joy Miller

ORISON
BOOKS

ISBN: 978-0-9964397-7-0

Orison Books
PO Box 8385
Asheville, NC 28814
www.orisonbooks.com

Distributed to the trade by Itasca Books
1-800-901-3480 / orders@itascabooks.com

Manufactured in the U.S.A.

ORISON
BOOKS

CONTENTS

III.

ACKNOWLEDGMENTS

Thanks to the editors of the following journals, where some of these poems first appeared, sometimes in different forms or with different titles:

The Adroit Journal: "Letter to Body Made Mineral," "Letter to Body Made Shadow," "Nightshift as Horsebride," and "Nightshift as Doppelgänger"

Blackbird: "Colony"

Bone Bouquet: "Dayshift Caught in the Ribs" and "Midshift Contemplating the Heart"

Boston Review: "Dayshift as Conduit"

burntdistrict: "Ceremonial: Heart of the Trottered Beast"

Cactus Heart Press: "I've always been the girl in the wrong"

Devil's Lake: "Nightshift as Slaughter"

Four Chambers Press: "Tikvah" and "The Break"

Gulf Coast: "Threnody for the Goat's Spine"

Linebreak: "Letter to Body Made Water"

Memorious: "War Song" and "Why You Tried to Drown"

Meridian: "Dream Ladder"

Midwestern Gothic: "We Followed the River's Loud Noise"

Muzzle Magazine: "On Crying Wolf"

Pinwheel: "Ceremonial Psalm"

Rock & Sling: "To Form a Prayer"

Ruminate: "Apostle" and "Apostle Delivers in the Kitchen"

The Shallow Ends: "Ceremonial in the Mouth of Desire"

Sixth Finch: "Girl Gone Vile: Portrait"

Souvenir: "Let the record show I was kind with the pick-axe hovered low by my thigh"
        and "Trouble"

Tahoma Literary Review: "Simone's Refrain as Apocalyptic Ballad"

Third Coast: "Anti-Pioneer"

Tinderbox Poetry Journal: "How ugly I've grown"

Tupelo Quarterly: "Weathered Porch"

Vinyl Poetry: "He Leaves Me to Run Horses" and "Lost Girl Wails Swan Song"

West Branch: "Ceremonial for the Beast I Desired"

Zocalo Public Square: "Letter to Body Made Breath"

"Girl Gone Vile: Portraiture," "Weathered Porch," "Why You Tried to Drown," and "War Song" were reprinted in *Poetry International.*

All poems titled "Dayshift," "Midshift," or "Nightshift," along with "Ceremonial: Heart of the Trottered Beast" and "Threnody for the Goat's Spine," also appear in *Like a Beast,* which won the 2016 Rick Campbell Chapbook Prize and is available from Anhinga Press.

Thank you to the editors at *Vinyl Poetry* for nominating "Lost Girl Wails Swan Song" for a 2016 Pushcart Prize. Thanks, too, to the editors at *Meridian,* where "Dream Ladder" was a finalist for the

2015 Editors' Prize.

Thank you to the University of California, Irvine, for the Creative Writing Emphasis—to the tutelage of Susan Davis, Colette LaBouff Atkinson, and Michael Ryan. An endless amount of gratitude to San Diego State University: to Sandra Alcosser, Marilyn Chin, and Ilya Kamisnky for their warmth, their brilliance, and encouraging wildness. Thank you Amanda Fuller, Jenny Minniti-Shippey, Katie Fagan, Carolann Caviglia Madden, Erin Rodoni, and Piotr Florczyk for reading versions of this manuscript, and to Dani Heinemeyer, Daniela Sow, Danielle Hunt, Garrett Bryant, Hari Alluri, Jeeae Chang, Jen Lagedrost, Karla Cordero, Katie Goudey, Kevin Dublin, Luke Crane, Lynn Wang, Michael Luke Benedetto, Rachel Gellman Martin and Victor Vazquez for support from afar. Forever thank you to Dave Rhei for sharing in this joy—all heart.

Thank you to the New York Summer Writers Institute, the Juniper Summer Writing Institute, and the *Tin House* Summer Workshop for time and focus.

To Henri Cole, Timothy Donnelly, and Natalie Diaz, thank you for spurring the conversations that kept these poems going. To Anna Rose Welch, Carlie Hoffman, Grady Chambers, Jia Oak Baker, Keegan Lester, Lauren Gordon, Meg Wade, Meghan Privitello, MK Foster, Peter LaBerge, Ruth Madievsky, and Leah Umansky for being continuous touchstones. To Analicia Sotelo, Eloisa Amezcua, Kaveh Akbar, Leslie Sainz, Luisa Muradyan Tannahill, Paige Lewis, and Tiana Clark, whose works and selves are full of wonder—thank you for your friendships, and to the joys in hello.

To Lisa Fay Coutley, who encouraged me to turn a corner. To Maggie Smith, who helped polish what I found there.

To Jay and Kristine Snodgrass—thank you for bringing the beast into the world, and for all Anhinga Press does.

To Carl Phillips—forever indebted, forever grateful that you chose *Ceremonial* for the 2017 Orison Poetry Prize.

To Luke Hankins, for all the beautiful work you do with Orison Books.

To my family—Mom, Dad, Stefanie, Lindsey—thank you for loving this poet lady. To an extended family of dear hearts: Aileen Itallo, Danielle Tackoor, Elif Poyrazoglu, Felicia Cheng, Gabrielle Doria, Kari Luu, Leilani Chaco, Michael Baum, and Michael Cho, for reading and laughing alongside me. To those I may have forgotten, thank you for your grace and continued love despite my memory. And to Grammy, love skyward.

FOREWORD

Here is the poet who knows the sensual art of speaking in tongues.

But what does it mean, in 2018, to speak in tongues? What *are* the spells of our moment? How do young poets of this arrogant late empire conjure their omens? What kind of ceremonials do they possess? What are the swan songs of their wreckage?

Carly Joy Miller often begins her poems with the seduction of tone: she is playful and ruinous at the same time. "I have always been the girl in the wrong / clothes for spring," she starts the poem, in a matter-of fact tone. "Last week I hunted the blond boys / who hunted a doe." That catches the eye. But what follows is working on a much deeper, stranger register: "I let out a dry cry. / Only the worms could hear me. / I've been that low." What a curious marriage of O'Hara and Plath! And Amy Gerstler! And the Witches' words in *Macbeth*!

The reader who opens this book on any random page will no doubt be delighted by its bravura, by its wish "to be the big bright bitch full of darkness," its prayer that "God shock the girl for getting something right. / Kill from the chandelier with a pearl strand. Swing the lights." This is the kind of tone and detail that wakes one up in the sleepy woods of contemporary American poetry. But what follows, as the pages turn, is far more interesting: a deep kind of time-travel, a swoon. Take the marvelous poem, "Weathered Porch," for instance:

> When my grandmother fell through
> the floorboards, she cupped her hands

to create an echo that crosses
five acres of cows, and they don't know how

to listen. Cows don't know how to move
closer in open fields. They need

whispers in their ears. Branding irons
or cracked whips taught them

how pain sounds—a bellow
from the fourth stomach. When her throat

dried, she settled for listening.
What she heard before having a body:

the rumbling of dirt, shuffling
of the many-headed rush,

a voice calling *I'm sorry* over
the cows' shuffling weight.

"What she heard before having a body"—this is the kind of a moment when one realizes that lively entertainment has turned into something transformative: a story become a myth. Or, take another wonderful lyric, "Apostle":

When water presses tightly to your ear

and your body seizes, do not panic.
I do not strike in the same place twice. Hear
how your breath staggers, turns manic
like the twelve-year-old boy who drowned
by the dock last March. His bones were not dense
enough to beat up from the algaed ground.
My voice is only as steady as the fencepost
cross that marks his jump. There would be nowhere
safe if I did not respect the living's space
where the roots hit the edges of the creek.
I take one, leave two for grieving. Now slow down
your prayer, and carry this message: I've spun
his body into tulips, taught him to swim and speak.

This signature Miller blend of tenderness and violence, this quest to "fable me along the wicked / spine," this account of "how frost hums for bone," is uncommon; it isn't yet another fairy-tale -influenced poem from an anthology of many contemporary fairy-tale-influenced poems. There is an act of wrenching that takes place here, something is visibly at stake—something sharp. And yet this sharpness, this terror, is, somehow, delicate. So "violence / flashes like thunder / and quakes on the walls."

Reading this book, one is often stirred by the boldness: "I begged the officer / to let me tango in churches / as an act of confession." One is delighted by the dualism of sensuality and tone: "The girl challenged the boy's mouth. / Instead of tongue, thumbs— / rubbed his molars / until they shined silver / with filling." One is compelled by the discovery: "He cannot shut his eyes from the dark / machine of the world." Seeing the sheer animism and sexual undertones of some of these poems, one can't help but think of James Dickey's "The Sheep Child" and Brigit Pegeen Kelly's *Song*. But the truly new song here is "War Song," and its clashing, worried, consoling syntax is all Carly Joy Miller's own: "Forgive my country, bread. / Forgive how I, under your nose, live: / how I, like the horse's tongue, / speak, how I / in the smudge and fray of ribs / and among thighs, breathe. // Forgive, life." That is *it*, the spell-like incantation.

And, when one thinks one's *got it*, one is surprised by being drawn in by the book's other kind of intimacies, sometimes frightful. Consider, for instance, "Why You Tried to Drown":

> Little soul, pulled
> down like a drum. Hook-line.
>
> Sinker. You swore there was gold
> at the bottom of the lake,
>
> swore the lake wanted you
> to wear its mossy skirt.
>
> Yes, you looked gorgeous,
> moths pitched white
>
> as barrettes in your hair.
> Little air, little sediment-coated
>
> tongue. Holy Nothing is a trickster:

oh to be young, yes young,

and lopsided in faith.

To be young and lopsided in faith—not a kind of prayer one would expect from the young poet in any age, nevermind 2018. And yet, here it is, the surprise of discovery. The new voice which is instantly recognizable as that rarest of occurrences: *the real thing.*

–Ilya Kaminsky

Your world has broken upon me like a flood.

—Rabindranath Tagore

I.

Dayshift as Conduit

My mother told me I live
like a beast and like a beast

I will die. So goes the omen:
my family tree rooted in animal

language: my bird-talk, my moth-cloths
stained with wings and petrichor.

I'm still slow
in old ways.

Close the blinds: my head
spins like a blade.

My head
is a grief

prison. Its one light,
an orb: my brother

buzzing, my dead brother full of teeth
and ache. Such is the gesture

of vision: so far into the dark
the past careens the dream until the dream

brands itself
as fate. My brother:

a blued body
to begin with: never

breathing, yet fell from my mother
all the same. Like a ghost, he paws

my doors of vision.
Like a beast, he grieves.

I've always been the girl in the wrong

clothes for spring, yet I understand my body
is a gift. I've not withered away. When my mother slaps
my thighs to circulate the water in the blood,
the bruises still purple. I let blood work
itself small again. Last week I hunted the blond boys
who hunted a doe in mist. We all saw the mother
gnawed to bone in upturned soil. I let out a dry cry.
Only the worms could hear me.
I've been that low.

Lost Girl Wails Swan Song

He saw me with cassette ribbons
laced around my fingers in the hay field.
Don't ask what put me there
fifteen years ago. Ask the wolves on the border.
Ask the hunter why moonshine
raised his aim high to my heart.
My sweater—left behind. My parents pried
carrion beetles so forensics could steal
a swatch of blood. I'm also
the shoe, laceless in the corn field.
When I think of everything I've lost,
I rejoice. No soap to scrub the devil
from my tongue, no belt to bruise
my wrists over a broken dish.
My parents think the day they buried me,
they laid two ghosts to rest—
mine choked in a casket, the killer's
to rot. To grieve is to
pound a knife along the mason
jar, already opened. Face it—
nobody wants to wake cruel.

There are always killings in the quiet
          line of trees. Trust in this:
wings sprouted from my shoulder blades.
          I glide on water.

Ceremonial Psalm

Blessed art the wild boys
who cross reveries, all sweet
milk, sweet tongues.
Leave them, small as pins,
under a sky that folds
like an eyelid.
A kiss quicks a valley
of thirst, and Lord, never
let them thirst.
Must I saint
myself at the altar
of your thighs, house
your sweat, cross
myself three times before
bells chime for more
salt? Wound me instead.
With no music left,
play metal and dust
along my false ribs.
Measure my years in plums
and water, stones

and fire. In grief.
            River my grief.
Blessed art the drowned
            boys, shot
boys, boys with shoulders
            wide as wandering
albatross. In fable,
            hours drear on
with no sound.
            Wound me into a thousand
clouded rooms occupied
            with boys I could love.
If not for restraint.
            If not for whims.
Each boy creases
            his room, mercies
a corner in waiting.
            Each lover I name
Lord. Each Lord a new
            ceremonial of wings.

Girl Gone Vile: Portrait

A kind of winning, to be the big bright bitch full of darkness.
Don't look at me that way. Weren't you proud when I came
home with an earful of dirt and a leech brass-knuckled
through my fingers? Didn't you love how gentleman I was
to throw my coat on the ground knowing there were so many
latched parts the girl with the pointiest jellies would trip?
That's fashion, honey. This is where you expect me to regret
skirts I wore at the playground so instead of sky, boys previewed
the underbelly they would grow to desire. Or not. How about
the time I pulled a bag over my head to know what movies meant
by loving someone completely without suffocating them?
Don't blink in disbelief. My nakedness is nothing holy.
God shock the girl for getting something right.
Kill from the chandelier with a pearl strand. Swing the lights.

Anti-Pioneer

with the goldsmith's braid whipped loose over
her hips—how permanent the smirk, the stench
of river between her knees. I know

what she's done: fastened mackerel to fashion
a skirt, ruffled the bear, called him brother,
called out brother in all the common

tongues. Fixed oscillations for any man
flecked with salt. How sensual: my wish
for the fish-dress to be mine, the buttonwoods

all mine. How sick to want the sages
drowsy with country-neglect. This is not
the dream tattered with frost, azury

with the flies hammered out of the ice.
This is where the wild fluttered out
as soon as I staked the land as mine.

Weathered Porch

When my grandmother fell through
the floorboards, she cupped her hands

to create an echo that crosses
five acres of cows, and they don't know how

to listen. Cows don't know how to move
closer in open fields. They need

whispers in their ears. Branding irons
or cracked whips taught them

how pain sounds—a bellow
from the fourth stomach. When her throat

dried, she settled for listening.
What she heard before having a body:

the rumbling of dirt, shuffling
of the many–headed rush,

a voice calling *I'm sorry* over
the cows' shuffling weight.

Fable

Boy broke his leg on a pine tree. Collapsed swanlike.
And he wanted to. He was only ten. Snapped twigs with his leg.
Police released hounds when he didn't come home.
Hounds love the smell of crushed elderberries and winter.
He was gazing at hoarfrost. How hoarfrost
resembled his own foggy breath. How cold it was.
It made the lake blush silver. And his girl was drifting
on the lake. Drift meaning glide. Glide meaning her skate
caught part of the lake and she tripped. It could have been worse.
She could have fallen in. Skate could catch latent
weedgrass, a fish's rib. Of course he wanted to check
if she was all right. He saw her rise up. He didn't care.
A duty's a duty. He found his calling. Boy broke
his leg on a pine tree. He climbed up there to watch
winter set a scene. Who knows how long it took him
to balance on a branch. And what time he began.
He climbed a long way to fall that quickly.
Wind offered no rustling. Wind offered no hollow

tunnel to carry his cry for help. That was his suffering
to deal with. The girl got up and reclaimed her balance.
She went on to the stronger part of the lake.
If she'd only looked up, she would have seen him
fall through branches. She could have saved him,
but that was not her duty. She could have mistaken
his quick fall for a hunted dove. Her heart
would break more for the dove. Red the round
elderberry in her hand. Red the blood on wing or knee.
It's all the same. Girl doesn't know how
to save something broken. She can only move on.
Cry one tear if she is quick enough
to wipe it away. It could freeze on her cheek
and she doesn't need a mark for loss
visible on her face. The sun fell. She thought
of a swan tucking beak into wing. That's
what all days must be like. All fall gracefully.
She was mistaken. If she'd just looked up
she could have saved him. Someone else
will find him. Someone else will drag him home.

Dayshift as Neighborhood Pariah

The first thing I ask the high-noon
        wolves when I question how the outskirted beg:

      What do I do with the thread
          of mother's pearled eye?

        What was I to do
            with lightning,
                all those volts
                    handed over

                    handed over
                the mop bucket
          her hair damp with soap.
        What was I to do?

The air heaves a gospel:

      The lagoon birthed orphans
      of fish, now scaled and weighed—

who doesn't want skin jeweled from the start?

Who else can I be?

Hush, hush, your little paws.
Rush me with answers, jowls.

Ceremonial for the Beast I Desired

His name biblical: Lord,
Apricot, Bougainvillea.

Nothing delights more
than his horns.

How they rouge me.
I raise my shirt in fête,

a stream of ribbons
storms his mouth.

Tragic, how ceremonies
bitter: my body a door

always closing.
Beast, when done,

blurs my chest still:
missed shadow, phantom

gift. Still I kiss
his jaw wild with yellow

jackets. I shepherd
too long in his furs.

On Crying Wolf

I am mad
as the lamb in a wolf's throat
and must be forgiven.
I'm over the idea of surrender,
how the lamb bleats
to nothing. The grass bends
with dewed blood on its bladetips.
There will be no grave
for the helpless—
so help me not.
I'll bury the wolf
deep into the woodchips,
deep as the promise
I must make to myself:
run. Gather my legs
in a slingshot and rush
till no one hears my rustling
on the ground.

Letter to Body Made Shadow

or criminal framed transparent
in the belly of a sunlit beast.

What to steal
with your scuffed

mouth and lopsided tongue?
There are no teeth to you.

Silent as carvers' knives
on the table—hush, listener,

this is a sacrificial act. Always
reduced to feet, my hooligan

shroud. Quiver beneath
the brow, your tongue tipped

with arrowheads for sour
blood. What spree—a lone bulb

you wish to bite. There are no
knives in your back, thank

goodness. What keeps you
tacked to me, my lone

saint of weeds? Maggot—
I mean, may we get

comfortable as suspects
or each other. May we slink

and croon across shrines with our soft
bodies. Our shoes, stones.

Dayshift Caught in the Ribs

To crash into the architecture
of the beast is to remember
how the body is rigged:

fable me along the wicked
spine and I trip
pearlescent. A bruise.

A wonder: how sea
glasses the ribs:
windows, paneling

a horn of light.
A chill. Day
airs me

like a sin
left to mercy:
how frost hums for bone.

II.

The Break

Let's examine the wreckage:

cracked bottle-caps   black hair clogging the weeds

                          my lover crooked on the scuffed-up creek.

Searchlights wreck the night's invitation for darkness.

                          So what of the mouth?

                                    Hunger-musked. Macabre.

          My eyes blinking but not—

                          a flutter from the water.

          Keep telling me to look down

                          as if I'll find something violent in the mud.

          Tell me we still have something to search for till dawn.

Why You Tried to Drown

Little soul, pulled
down like a drum. Hook-line.

Sinker. You swore there was gold
at the bottom of the lake,

swore the lake wanted you
to wear its mossy skirt.

Yes, you looked gorgeous,
moths pitched white

as barrettes in your hair.
Little air, little sediment-coated

tongue. Holy Nothing is a trickster:
oh to be young, yes young,

and lopsided in faith.

Apostle

When water presses tightly to your ear
and your body seizes, do not panic.
I do not strike in the same place twice. Hear
how your breath staggers, turns manic
like the twelve-year-old boy who drowned
by the dock last March. His bones were not dense
enough to beat up from the algaed ground.
My voice is only as steady as the fencepost
cross that marks his jump. There would be nowhere
safe if I did not respect the living's space
where the roots hit the edges of the creek.
I take one, leave two for grieving. Now slow down
your prayer, and carry this message: I've spun
his body into tulips, taught him to swim and speak.

Midshift Contemplating Genius

Another slaughter. Blur of my longing as stars ribbon another bright trick: flies don, not jewel, rot. Sweetness still lingers in the basin: taste your fingers. Reason, a hand of god: sweetness an unthinking harm.

Letter to Body Made Water

This is my striving
for other chances to break

you at the hips. Lust
is admirable. But there's a flood

about you. You notice
I've secured the heart

on wire racks to watch it beat
like a bell. I notice

the damn cry, mid-afternoon.
The window bothered with streak

and shine. I'm sorry. I tried to swim
the throat of you. That only bruises

and startles the horses.
My own violence

flashes like thunder
and quakes on the walls.

Simone's Refrain as Apocalyptic Ballad

The girl challenged the boy's mouth.
            Instead of tongue, thumbs—
rubbed his molars

            until they shined silver
with filling. She pearled
            her lunula with his gums.

You know what I mean.
            The one pinned down
on the floor may have been

            the one who touched first.
Who's to say when the breeze
            drifts by, it's not able

to lie with the pine
            without a scream to set it off.
You're thinking terror—

            you should hope for pleasure.

There's been a small death
        out back. There's no blood.

The skirt's skid up.
        You know how I feel
with splinters trapped

        in my back. And his.
Who never said the girl was me.
        You placed me outside

with sun spooning
        my calves till they warped
tan, desirable. The birds

        hover low. They want
to pick bones for flesh
        when we're ripe

and dead. Is there a swelling
        that stiffens you
in the doorway

        of celebration?
Are you too bothered

to move?

Colony

Bees curl dead beside the swimming pool,
wings clipped as a straight-stitch seam.
We tiptoe coldly from the water. Of course

we hover, make a colony.

> They sense fear, sweat lacquered
> on our lips. We tuck
> our susceptible legs.

The bees curl, offer
   their deaths to evening.
         Slowness a blessing
               on the body's horizon.

We relish that small silence,
               a hot star, fixed station
of revolution.

Yet the bees curl dead:
in clumps they are

                              not bees

but stigmas, loose bulbs of pollen
                dancing, ghosting the air
                        with a last bit of sun.

This is the body: take it or not. Yes, the body falls. Of course: we are meant for dents. Of course: we shiver in grief. Of course: try to shake up some glimmer of light. Turn ourselves loose on the wind.

And we fear.
Of course we should.

Prayer spits out of our lips and we send it skyward,
knock on the gray doors of our lives.

Let the record show I was kind with the pick-axe hovered low by my thigh

I begged the officer
            to let me tango in churches
                        as an act of confession.

He didn't stand long. I bleached his chambray shirt
            to construct a proper signal
                        for surrender. That doesn't mean

I didn't spit. I begged him to drown me in the river
            and be fished out nameless—
                        faux-baptism for the girl

who quit rage. The war against the body
            is over. Now I want to thrust my hands
                        into the earth—press my wildness low.

Tikvah

I cannot promise angels but I can
promise I've held many things

pot handles handles of mirrors if
you want to see yourself clearly

look to water bend your knees 45 degrees
tilt your head say *ahh* so the reflecting

light can travel down to your
belly you only absorb good

words good prayers whispers that wait
for the right shade of grief to stick

you into mud I have been there many
times have told fables to claim lives

I have not lived outside of this body
that binds me that drifts to open palms

of many saviors even the crusts
of bread I consider holy walls

if you must tear them down do it now
break your bones if you want to be saved

save yourself but if you want me
to sing I will sing.

To Form a Prayer

Decide to bend a little.

Train your ear for a voice
that will not crease.

Do not slouch with a fervor
under your belly.

No one swarms to the desperate.

Your face veiled
with doubt.

Kiss your fingers
with pursed lips. Stop.

Do not give into
a drowning.

Bees hum in your molars.
Warrant them out.

Midshift Contemplating the Heart

Unfaced unlimbed so only center: where will you spread your rust, my beaut? Tasseled begonia, scarlet hummer, my little psalm doll: hollow be thy head when I pang you again. Apologies: the ones I love loot my cage. Their appetites curl the girl right out of me.

Ceremonial: Heart of the Trottered Beast

Little elbow of pleasure
in the eating dress.

The animal needs room,
unchurched

yet beautiful. I never
considered the cathedral

a body needing to break.
I laid the trottered down.

Pestle the eyes, opaque
in vision. As soon as

I take the cloth to clean
the sockets, the organs play

their last bright notes.
Terrible the sounds

of gobbledom.
Slice the gut. Dig

the ticking thing out:
Sacrament. Blood lyre.

I wipe my tongue of it.

Dream Ladder

My body does the haunting:

> rusts the hinges, spares

> > with its coy self.

With *hinge*, I want to say

> *wrist* or *knee* or *corner*

> > yet here I am, babbling

on a dry-eyed rung.

> > > *

> Lord, with my dress like air,

> > I'm all cellar and legs.

With loose thread

I cast myself like

                                        I am the boy's

again. All that height

                    I gripped. All that

                                        flesh I gripped.

And all that mouth

                    under all that mouth, I drowned.

                              *

                                        Correct me boy:

in my hour of missing,

                    how did you want to discover me?

                                        Laughing, my obelisk

legs bound to the floor? *No,*

        that's not how haunting works.

                  Correct me boy:

when I pulled you into blue

        couches lining the cellar,

                  did your ribs whistle

themselves into honey? *No.*

        Lover-boy, you are not

                  kind.

You cannot correct me on this one.

              *

        My tiny

fists snag his

chest. The boy's

    voice collapses between

        one rung or another.

Pangs like piss

    in a bedpan. I need

        to shut him up.

What's a girl to do

    with lips crisp

        as apples besides bruise?

*

Cellar: dream sign

of neglect. And levels:

a sign of wakefulness.

How awake were you, boy,

when I stormed

my own palm for signs?

Even my fingers,

like I knew my prints

on a smudged water glass.

Lie still, I say,

lie still and never wake.

This silence needs

to ripen.

The fruit it bears

is my own breasts.

Graceless flopovers—

I can only be human

a short, short time.

*

Lord, I've traced

this corner's dust

so long. *It's night, sugar. Drag*

yourself to another side.

*

To climb a ladder

is prayer. To climb down:

a season of gulls,

a crumpled fable.

*

And I'm the one to destroy

a good thing.

May I harden

like a gourd. Lose my arms

and not flinch.

Lose my tongue

to bees so they

sing my sighs.

*

The boy is neither enemy

nor dead. Nor stranger.

I don't recognize

who I hover over.

His arms accordions, how

they retract

to the living.

I cannot live here.

I am only ghost

a short, short time.

III.

Letter to Body Made Breath

Long rivulet of me
strikes the ram's horn.

My name hymns
god-bright in the lungs:

Loosen me,
revenant. Your absence

caused me to crawl in
the low fields

like a woman in war.
All that labor.

I've made a myth of it.
Dress billow-whips

my knees. Breathe:
body arch. Breathe:

body flutter. Breathe:
we linger. At the end

of anything, a lift.
Believe or leave

a breath—

Nightshift as Horsebride,

meaning bridled, although
    my gown in this
rawhide desire
    tulled above the knee

wounds. Soft scrape, bruises,
    a brush of hay.
I barefoot toward my lover
    turned groom

turned handler.
    Bridled: how I raise
my head, a bucket
    full of salt. How I bite cheeks

of pears to jerk
    fallacy from my mouth.
Debridement: the harness
    snaps in your fist,

eschar violets before

       the kiss. Fallacy:
my gums
       gleam in moonlight.

The milked-out stars
       swoon at my flank,
hiplatched
       gate swinging.

He Leaves Me to Run Horses

and all I know are the seventy manes
found in autumn's good graces:

chestnut, auburn, coal, ash.
And all the tiny hairs fall

on my jeans and collarbone.
I arrange them on a pillow.

Still, I am disappointed
with how I weave your body

back into this bed. Never again
shall I gather oleander and wool

with crochet hooks. Never tie
nettles with corn silk and soak

the mixture in wax and milk.
The heart tumbles until it splits

from *yes*. Still, I hear only hooves.

Ceremonial in the Mouth of Desire

He cannot shut his eyes to the dark
machine of the world. I cannot release

my hips from the holy grip hoisting me up
or pulling low. Not his hands, this man

beside me. Little stranger, tender as a bride.
No. This man marks me with his mouth.

Animal how he moves toward the din
of hunger. Devourment, a dedication.

War Song

Forgive my country, bread.
Forgive how I, under your nose, live:

how I, like the horse's tongue,
speak, how I
in the smudge and fray of ribs
and among thighs, breathe.

Forgive, life, how
crumpled
doily
your body was.
Forgive my country,
your armory, the bread of war.

Nightshift as Slaughter

Hallelujah I'm purposed.

My bits lording the dirt,

weather a stain around

the high grasses. Gone the season

of kneeling to my femur

—or is it my humerus, some meat

graying the bone? Dark laughter

behind me—these steps, these paws,

I know them all. Amen for fright,

the gaudy shriek. The gauze

of new hair over me, amen.

Apostle Delivers in the Kitchen

You wake in a fry-pan
room, sun slapping your skin red. This happens
to everyone. What you have longed for, yes,
I will give you. Dust yourself with pollen
then set yourself to shackling
tongues in other mouths to understand
silence. Land on the roof and be attentive:
this is the hour babies sleep, the hour
of pressing weight onto another
for pleasure. It pleases you. Even with him
gone, touch pleases you. Your skin
marbled, the kitchen counter
blue-veined. Welcome back
to coolness. Rest in it.

We followed the river's loud noise,

our map
        my father's right palm—
palm led us to gravesides, lifeline
        to corn-husked fields. Each stalk
flopped when burdened. His loveline went
        with each husk, fine wisps
of silk that must be chopped.
        His hair, a thin crown,
covered his sun-blistered head. God's hand
        pats closely to the scalp, will choose when
        it is time to pull him up, leave us to shuck his clothes,
        thresh the thousand
        kernels of his body.
        My father's sleep
        sleep
        silted deep in bourbon bottles.
        The amber glass lights
        the cottonweed, the burrs

tangle our hair.
What river savages we
become, and are not afraid
of tempering.

Trouble

I leave, mistake a bird's broken

leg for twig

hidden in the curt cloud-shadows.

The berries in my hand

may save or silence me. In my silence

I strip my clothes like the world is my house.

Moss, lush carpet, body

the dry earth, and all

doorhinges and rusted circuits

stain and spread a copper sheen.

The sky, my dark ceiling.

Nightshift as Doppelgänger

Born hellish, hooves and tress.
　　To be slick, I jellied my insides out.
　　　　My heart plummish to enamor rot.
　　　　　　To be your other.

　　　　　　Ever brief.
　　　　Accept me—your strange shadow.
　　　　　Tenet of the tramp dress.
　　　　　　　Shiner.
　　Loose me to a field
　　　　and place a mirror beside me.
　　Loose me to a field
　　　　and scythe my chest open
　　　　　　　to three crestfallen horses,
　　　　　　　　to opal,
　　　　　　　　　to evening
　　　　　　　　　　varnished in skein.
　　　　　　　　　To plum-reek.

To hooked
　　　bones purled.

How ugly I've grown

into a forgetfulness. I've lost my manners
because drought has taken all the glassware
from my cupboard and I can't gesture water.
But love, if you want to go
wild in the china shop
of my body, do.
I warn you, I am an idiot
at touch. You don't believe me—
look at the hydrangeas.

Letter to Body Made Mineral

Is your mouth a crater in this country too?
And do you smell medicinal as you pry

hemlock apart in your study
of nerves? When you spring

nettles in a puddle of water,
do they point toward the god you

should pine over next? Tell me you sway
like molasses in summer. Tell me how

you dropped to your knees as if to pray
when the gun ricocheted in your hands.

Isn't the bullet just a magnet
for iron in blood? Who are the ghosts

falling beside you and are they yours

for haunting? Who straightjackets

your arms to your small back
so you grovel less alone? Is your mother

overbearing with all her white dresses?
Do you agree tongues grate like saws when

spitting truths every hour? Noiseful burden.
How do you contour your afternoons

so they lay flat on your stomach
as you practice sacrificing yourself

to wolves and doves alike?
What were you aiming at

with that gun in your hands?
When we fall, we fall like gravel

with shoulders bruised terribly human.

Threnody for the Goat's Spine

The old lover appears, fully
naked. It is winter. His coat
nowhere beside him. I search
the footpath, war with the dark

silt. Nothing. Before I speak,
I clear birds from my throat.
He stands in the tower
of his body, waits.

I oil a lantern, press it to my belly.
Watch it flatten. Nightjars
 appear, blackened with thirst.
They soar to the barn, unhinge

the latch with their beaks.
The lover and I stand
in the doorway and watch

them clench the goat's teat.

She goes limp without milk.
Nightjars loosen their throats
and spit enough to bless
the burn on my belly. I bless

the goat with an axe. It creaks
between the head and neck,
thirty-one vertebrae of spine. I break
everything. I create room enough

for the lover to enter
the goat's coat. He opens
his mouth wide enough
for me to crawl in and speak.

ABOUT THE AUTHOR

Carly Joy Miller's work has appeared in *The Adroit Journal, Blackbird, Boston Review, Gulf Coast, West Branch*, and elsewhere. She is a contributing editor at *Poetry International* and a founding editor of Locked Horn Press. Her chapbook *Like a Beast* won the 2016 Rick Campbell Prize and was published by Anhinga Press in 2017.

ABOUT ORISON BOOKS

Orison Books is a 501(c)3 non-profit literary press focused on the life of the spirit from a broad and inclusive range of perspectives. We seek to publish books of exceptional poetry, fiction, and non-fiction from perspectives spanning the spectrum of spiritual and religious thought, ethnicity, gender identity, and sexual orientation.

As a non-profit literary press, Orison Books depends on the support of donors. To find out more about our mission and our books, or to make a donation, please visit www.orisonbooks.com.